Contents

A Quick Guide To Dealing With Burnout Syndrome

Valentin Boyadzhiev

Introduction

Dear Ladies and Gentlemen, this book, "A Quick Guide to Dealing With Burnout Syndrome", was created specifically to introduce readers to the basic concepts and insights surrounding Occupational Exhaustion Syndrome. The book claims neither completeness nor absolute comprehensiveness, but I dare to say that it is an indispensable helper to anyone struggling with stress or Burnout Syndrome. It is useful for both the victim and anyone who has a loved one suffering from this condition. The syndrome conquers all major areas of human existence and functioning. It is not only a personal problem, it is a problem of modern society and it affects not only the individual and his life but also everyone close to him. I tried to create a light, concise, and enjoyable book that would provide every reader with something interesting and accessible from this wide and vast field of scientific knowledge. The book explains and presents the basic concepts and phenomena associated with Burnout Syndrome, explores some basic theories about the formation, evolution, and ways of coping with this condition. I wish you a pleasant and useful minute with this book. Thank you for your attention and interest. Best wishes, Valentin Boyadzhiev!

About the author

Valentin Boyadzhiev is a trained nutritionist, graduated Master of Psychology in "Psychology and Psychopathology of Development". He has acquired Professional Qualification "Teacher of Psychology" and Postgraduate Professional Qualification "Psychological Counseling in Psychosomatic and Social Adaptation Disorders". He has obtained a Psychoanalysis Diploma and he has specialized in Psychoanalytic Psychotherapy. He is a member of the Association "Bulgarian Psychoanalytic Space", "International Society of Applied Psychoanalysis" and „International Alliance of Holistic

Therapists". He is a lecturer on issues related to nutrition, diet, supplementation, food and sports. He is also a teacher and a lecturer in the field of psychology, logic, ethics, law, and philosophy. He has been a school psychologist since 2017. He has been participating annually in scientific conferences on psychology, psychotherapy, dietetics and medicine. His main interest and practice are in the field of psychoanalysis and clinical psychology.

What is Burnout?

Burnout is a slang term for extreme emotional exhaustion, most expressed in terms of our work. Feelings such as apathy, lack of professional motivation, fit of anger, passive aggression and an overall feeling of frustration are typical. Stress makes us feel powerless, and the body logically responds to the anxiety of the mind with symptoms such as headache, high blood pressure and pain in the neck, waist and chest. Disturbed or deep sleep, problems with wakening or falling asleep are other common problems directly related to stress that can disrupt our natural balance.

Occupational Exhaustion Syndrome (Burnout Syndrome) is a term used in the 1974 article "*Burnout: The High Cost of High Achievement*" by American psychiatrist Herbert J. Freudenberger. He noticed this syndrome among his colleagues. It is defined by specific symptoms and stages of development.

The fundamental aspect of this syndrome is an increased sense of intellectual, emotional and physiological exhaustion. Without a strict definition, it is considered as an occupational phenomenon that affects all aspects of the personality - physiological, emotional, behavioural, including the manifestation of suicidal moods, stroke, heart attack, colitis, ulcer, gastritis, obesity, migraine, asthma, sterility. In recent years, research has expanded to include a wider range of professions - police officers, teachers, journalists, doctors, scientists, and more. According to a study by the National Association of General Practitioners, 70% of doctors in Bulgaria suffer from this syndrome.

Developing interests outside the workplace is recommended to counteract this occupational disease - something that is done with pleasure. In 1982, the American psychologist Christina Maslach, together with her colleague Susan E. Jackson, developed a scientific method to study the syndrome of occupational exhaustion, which created the first test to assess the level of Burnout: "Maslach

Burnout Inventory" "(MBI). The development of the syndrome is proportional to the mismatch between personality and profession. Christina Maslach identifies six basic areas of discrepancy:

1. Requirements for the employee and his real capabilities.
2. Striving for independence in work and the degree of the applied control.
3. Work effort and underestimation of contributions.
4. Absence of positive relationships with co-workers.
5. Absence of fair work relationships.
6. Ethical principles of personality and job requirements.

Psychology doctor Archibald Hart establishes certain differences between stress and occupational exhaustion syndrome that extend between physical hyperactivity and emotional exhaustion.

10 signs that you are close to a Burnout

Challenges at work are important - they awaken creativity and give a sense of satisfaction after being fulfilled. At the same time, they can be exhausting - if we do not reduce the pace they can lead to stress, loss of sleep and the feeling that we are drowning - no matter where we look - we always find a new problem that seems to have no solution. Burnout can take many forms, but they can all take us far away from the career and goals we dream to achieve. Here are some signs that you are close to

Burnout and what to do if you find them.

1. Avoiding difficult conversations

This is one of the hidden signs of a Burnout that becomes very apparent over time. Early signs are avoiding serious conversations and making decisions. To these can be added the incompletion of tasks that can lead to increased responsibilities and professional recognition.

2. Lack of concentration

If you stare aimlessly at your monitor and dream all day long, you might start to get into a Burnout. You are at work, but you are only there physically, you cannot concentrate and be productive. It's time to change your daily routine - start getting up early and exercising, get involved in a side project related to your passion, or change your office design.

3. You ask yourself "Am I getting into a Burnout?"

If you ask yourself this question, you may already be approaching this state. Burnout appears when we stop incorporating vital things into our daily lives. Discover the things you no longer spend time for and what you can do to get them back. Maybe it's a personal decision you have to make or boundaries you have to set. Ask for help if you need it.

4. Avoiding contact with people

If you don't have any desire for meeting people, phone calls, or general conversations, or don't want to get out of your desk at all, you might be close to a Burnout. It is common among professionals in the service sector because communicating with people requires genuine energy and dedication, whether you are an introvert or an extrovert. To avoid the fatigue of interacting with people, set up self-care habits such as meditation and healthy eating.

5. Hiding behind a mask

A common sign of Burnout is insincerity. If you are wearing a mask or are always trying to look energetic and joyful, it's time to face the real situation. If you cannot truly commit to your work, look for the cause within you. Make a list of your major values and ask yourself "What is the relationship between my work and my values?" Find ways to overlap them or look for new opportunities.

6. You have problems with engagement

If you find it difficult to get involved in projects or help colleagues, this may be a sign of a Burnout. To solve this, try to find the root cause and seek the support of colleagues, management, or contact a professional. Often, Burnout is due to too much work or a mismatch between profession and skills. Addressing the problem is important and helps to avoid depression or illness.

7. You are irritable

Irritability is a less commonly recognized symptom of Burnout. Your irritability targets your colleagues, work and even at home. It is a result from a sense of inefficiency and lack of competence in work and lack of purpose. When you feel irritated, take a step back and try to identify the cause. If the cause is a lack of purpose then try to find one for yourself.

8. You want to be on sick-leave

We may not be physically ill, but it could make us sick at the thought of returning to work. Consider the positives and negatives of your work environment, management and development opportunities. If negatives prevail, then it's time to look for a new job that nourishes your career, health and balance.

9. You're bored

As time goes by, creativity begins to drain your energy, make you irritated or even annoyed. Boredom is a real feeling and if you find yourself in this situation, first identify the part of your work that is boring you, then look for new ways to regain your previous enthusiasm. Restore creativity and love your work again.

10. You are frustrated and cynical

One of the many signs of Burnout is frustration and cynicism. Instead of ignoring them, stand up to the situation and start to see the benefits of it: if you had not experienced these feelings, you would not have asked yourself many essential questions. Find out what you value and what makes sense for you and strive for it.

Components of occupational burnout

According to psychologist Christina Maslach, one can recognize the Burnout in these 3 main components:

1. **Exhaustion** - This is a huge emotional, mental and physical fatigue that hinders our ability to be effective in our work. In this case, the level of fatigue is so big that even after a night of full sleep and rest, one cannot regain his or her strength because the energy deficiency from the Burnout is too big.

2. **Cynicism** - You may start to feel annoyed, irritable, and frustrated with work and your colleagues

3. **Inefficiency** - Evolve from a sense of incompetence and the fear of failure. You may feel that you cannot handle something or that there is no way to succeed.

Although there is a link between the different components, studies show that different people have a specific Burnout profile. For you, the predominant factor could be exhaustion, while others may have a sense of inadequacy in the situation.

Burnout stages

Getting into a Burnout is a lengthy process, it is not something that has a clear start and may not be recognized for this reason. You will also notice that some of the stages may seem unrelated directly to stress, while others may be considered as a normal part of the job. Getting into a Burnout is usually unnoticeable - which is why it can get so deep in it. After the red line (after the 9th stage) exit is impossible without outside help. If one person in the organization is in Burnout that shows the peculiarities of the environment and means that at least a few more of his colleagues have already started the same path.

1. The need of proving yourself.

Constant high need or its escalation for proving. The question may be raised whether this is related to good self-esteem.

2. Enhanced engagement with work responsibilities, including beyond direct obligations.

So far we see things that can even be encouraged by the organization. Here is a moment to remember that to hold one person responsible has two sides: the responsibility to others and the more important is the responsibility to oneself.

3. Neglecting the needs

Mostly neglecting the need for rest and recovery. Reducing time spent on family, privacy, hobbies, sports, etc.

4. Suppression of needs and conflicts

Suppression of internal and external contradictions that create proving and over-involvement. We may not "see" or "forget" our needs, emerging conflicts in the family, etc., but the suppression itself exacerbates their negative effects.

5. Reassessment of values in case of constant overload

If we conclude that work is more important than things that bother us and cannot be combined with them, the process is deepened. But a reassessment of values can also lead to de-socialization.

6. Enhanced denial of the emerged problems

The moment when not only the existing ones are suppressed, but the refusal to see what is currently happening in its entirety comes. It is also a refusal to see the real meaning of prooving and over-involvement. As we said, suppressing needs and conflicts increase their negative effects, and this reduces the capacity for work - the exact opposite of what is desired. Whether we realize this stage depends on how much we pay attention to the feedback we receive from others and our family. Again -

the organization may be interested in the person devoting more and more time to work and spending less time on other parts of his lives. That is why we say that the environment itself creates crucial conditions for a Burnout.

7. Emotional exhaustion and withdrawal

Debasing of capacity for work. The lifestyle has been changed to impede recovery and cause emotional exhaustion. One gets up in the morning for work, the stomach is on the ball, nothing foretells a good experience. This leads to a withdrawal. Additional withdrawal from privacy, but also withdrawal from obligations in which one cannot prove himself or is no longer capable of engaging.

8. Behavioural change

The sense of not coping is deepening. The sense of professional achievement is constantly diminishing. It occurs changes in behaviour such as coldness toward colleagues and those in charge (for example teacher to students), loss of sense of social belonging, cynicism.

9. Depersonalization

Loss of sense of one's own personality, loss of sense of the reality of experiences. Going through this 9th stage, we cannot save ourselves alone. There is a risk of suicide.

10. Internal emptiness

11. Depression

12. The complete exhaustion which is Burnout that will take years to recover.

10 Tips in case of Burnout

Burnout feeds on the energy, enthusiasm and passion of the best professionals, turning these qualities into exhaustion, nervousness and disappointment. The good news is that the Burnout can be overcome and this condition can be completely eliminated. Although it certainly requires a change in lifestyle, once you admit the existence of Burnout and work hard to overcome it, it can become a positive force in your life and an opportunity to reinvent yourself. If you are a victim of Burnout, here are some steps you can take to bring back the joy of your life and work and become yourself again.

1. Make a list of your difficult situations

Make a list of all work situations that make you feel stressed, anxious, worried, frustrated, angry, and/or helpless.

2. List ways to deal with each situation

In front of each difficult situation of your list write down at least one way to change it or to change your behaviour in order to reduce the anxiety. Then start applying this to your daily routine. Do not be disappointed if you do not feel immediate results. The Burnout doesn't happen overnight, so it's unrealistic to expect it to disappear so quickly.

3. Delegation

Delegate and transfer as much of your work as possible to your colleagues or subordinates, even if they do not deal with them as quickly or as well as you would.

4. Just say no

As you recover, avoid taking on new engagements or responsibilities. Yes, there will certainly be things that you will have to do (such as paying your bills). But this is another matter. Most of us have a bad habit of saying yes when they can just refuse. Resist this desire.

5. Be sure to rest between two tasks

Burnout weakens your mental and physical strength, so avoid jumping from one stressful, time-consuming task to another. Give your mind and body a chance to recover.

6. Control your electronic devices

Electronic devices (tablets, smartphones, laptops, etc.) consume a great deal of your energy, which in the state of Burnout is lacking anyway. To recover faster from Burnout - turn them off whenever possible.

7. Communicate with people outside your workplace

This will give you an outside viewpoint and a new perspective on life in general. Meet friends often and just have fun.

8. Do not work after working hours

Yes, we know that you have to do your job today and that is why you will continue to work tonight. But if you want to continue to be productive, efficient and above all healthy, you have to slow down the pace. Significantly. Arrange your priorities correctly and put yourself in the first place. Do not work all the time!

9. Try to sleep longer

Lack of sleep is a major factor in the occurrence of Burnout. Therefore, you need to take urgent steps to restore it. As we all know, "sleep is health". It is vital for you. If it is necessary you can try and change your habits to sleep at least 6-7 hours a day. Seek professional help if needed.

10. Exercise regularly

Aerobic exercise is preferred when recovering from a Burnout. Any activity that speeds up your pulse and loads your heart rate in fact, makes you more resistant to cardiovascular disease and significantly reduces the symptoms of Burnout.

Burnout recovery

Change your daily routine

Restructure your workday. Whether you are in motion at work or sitting behind a desk but still you feel stressed and exhausted, the most effective way to change it is to quit that job and find a new one you love and enjoy doing. Of course, changing jobs is far from being a practical and easily achievable solution - especially when you are grateful that you have a job thanks to which you can pay your bills and cover your daily expenses. Whatever the situation is, there is always something you can do to improve your state of mind.

Find the value in what you do

Even in the most ordinary and at first glance easy activities, you can find how and with what they help others, such as the necessary goods or services. Focus on the moments in your work that make you smile feel good - these can even be the conversations on all topics with your colleagues at lunch. Changing your perspective and attitude towards work can help you regain a sense of purpose and control.

Make friends at work

A strong workplace relationship can help reduce monotony and counteract the Burnout syndrome. Talking and joking with friends on a day-to-day basis can help ease the stress of failure or hard work, improve work efficiency, or just relax during a difficult day.

Find the balance in your life

If you hate your job, find meaning and satisfaction elsewhere in your life - family, friends or hobbies. Focus on that part of your life that brings you pleasure and positive emotions.

Become more selfish and set your boundaries

Don't give in too much. Learn to say no to requests and demands that limit your time for relaxation and the family. Exactly this "no" will allow you to say 'yes' to the things you really want to do. Take a day off from technology. Take the time to fully detach yourself from your laptop, phone, and email. If you spend most of your working time responding to the demands and wishes of others or only perform tasks that you have been instructed to do, the risk of Burnout is high. More and more leaders of successful companies are admitting the importance of giving their employees time to complete their projects, ideas and tasks. If you work in an office, focus on the most important and essential tasks in the morning, before the time for a lunch break. That way, you can take some time off at the end of the workday to manage to do something interesting, innovative, creative or just your favourite something. So, in small steps, every day, you can complete your personal project.

Feed your creative side

Creativity is among the most powerful antidotes to Burnout Syndrome. Try starting something new or revive your hobby. Choose an activity that has nothing to do with your work. Take time for relaxation. Techniques such as yoga, meditation, and deep breathing may be more useful than you think. Try it! Meditating for only about 10 minutes a day will contribute to increased concentration and improved mood. You can also meditate at your workplace.

View your successes and failures

Take the time at the end of the workweek to analyze all the difficulties and successes you have encountered during this period. Write down your goals and accomplishments. This will help you understand how you should proceed. You may even find a solution to a potential problem before it occurs. You can write down all your answers in the form of short notes in your notebook or use the note function in your phone. In fact, the idea is to separate yourself from the "battlefield" and look at your work from a distance. This way, you can break away from your problems and determine what you need to do to deal with them. And, if, despite all your efforts, you still feel close to the

Burnout, it might be a good idea to consider whether this is your professional career.

Improve your health

Help yourself through a healthy diet. Minimize sugar and refined sugars. Limit foods such as French fries, chips and sweets as they can lead to a collapse in mood and energy. Others that may negatively affect your mood include caffeine, trans fats, and foods containing preservatives or hormones. Take more omega-3 fatty acids to boost your mood. The best sources are fatty fish (salmon, herring, mackerel, sardines), seaweed, flaxseed and walnuts. Avoid nicotine. Smoking may seem soothing to you, but nicotine is a powerful stimulant, leading to higher levels of stress. Drink alcohol in moderation. Alcohol temporarily reduces anxiety, but too much can cause anxiety. Vitamins and supplements. Therapy with vitamins and supplements can help support the body with existing nutritional deficiencies. Daily stressors can lead to an increased need for certain nutrients. Often, in this case, high-quality multivitamins and minerals are recommended. There are also many herbs that can improve energy reserves and maintain immunity. Asian ginseng, Siberian ginseng, Ashwagandha are herbs that are commonly used to help the body adapt to stress. Each vitamin or herbal therapy should be discussed with your doctor in advance to determine if this supplement is necessary and, if so, whether the correct dosage is appropriate. Also, it is necessary to evaluate all possible interactions between herbs and medicines.

Get your sleep

The feeling of fatigue can exacerbate Burnout Syndrome and contribute to irrational thinking. Good night sleep is a powerful weapon against stress during the day.

Do exercises

Exercise may seem like the last thing you want to do when you are on the brink of Burnout, but in fact, it can greatly improve your mood. Try walking, running, swimming, dancing and even martial arts. Get together with friends and organize fitness days. With this, you will simultaneously have fun, relax and maintain tone and form. If you do not have a gym available, home workouts can also be extremely helpful. The goal is to exercise for 30 minutes or more once a day or to do several short, ten-minute series. Walking ten minutes on foot can improve your mood for two hours.

Take a break

If Burnout seems unavoidable, try to completely separate yourself from your work for a while. Take a vacation out of town, indulge in a hobby or to the family - no matter what you choose, it must bring you peace and joy. Use the time to recharge your batteries and think about the next steps to recover from Burnout.

Final Words

Thanks to all the readers who were interested in this book. I tried to make a brief and enjoyable synthesis of some of the most influential theories in psychology related to Occupational Exhaustion Syndrome. I hope that each of you is satisfied with the reading and has acquired new knowledge that will serve you both in work and life in general. I hope that each one of you will be able to obtain the needed knowledge from this short guide and successfully apply, if not every step described to deal with stress and syndrome, at least those that give you confidence in their ability to help. Best wishes, Valentin Boyadzhiev!

www.ingramcontent.com/pod-product-compliance
Lightning Source LLC
Chambersburg PA
CBHW051128250726
48655CB00007B/2942